I Like Pink Milk

Pauline Cartwright
Photography by
Lindsay Edwards

I like milk.
Mum likes milk.

I like strawberries.
Mum likes strawberries.

I like pink milk.
Mum likes pink milk.

I will make pink milk!
Mum will help.

I get the milk.
The milk is white.

I get the strawberries.
The strawberries are red.

In goes the white milk.

In go the red strawberries.

Mum will mix them.

The milk is pink.
Pink milk is yum!

I like yellow milk.
Can we make yellow milk?